Burmese Cats in Camera

by

Moira Swift

Robine Pocock

Christina Payne

Panther Photographic

Acknowledgements

The authors wish to thank the following people for their help and assistance in preparing the manuscript.

Miss Julie Welch, Mrs Hazel Dodgson, Mr Laurence Payne, Mr Hamilton Woods.

The authors are indebted to the owners of the Burmese Cats featured, without whose help this book would not have been possible.

First Published 1989

ISBN 0-9515400-0-9
Published by: Panther Photographic
Foxboro
East Wretham, Thetford, Norfolk, England

Picture Acknowledgements

Christina Payne	All black & white pictures, with the exceptions listed below.
Anne Cumbers	8, bottom right; 9, top; 10, top; 11, top; 17, middle, bottom; 19; 24, top right; 26, left bottom; 28; 35; 37, top right, bottom; 42; 43; 46, bottom.
Paul Bookbinder	7; 9, bottom; 46, top.
B.J. Harris	9, middle.
Robine Pocock	10, bottom; 16, bottom.
Paddy Cutts	16, top left.
Sarah Barton	17, top right.
Derek Davies	20, bottom left.
Lola Marsden	23.
Arthur Hance	47.
Panther Photographic	Colour plates, Front cover.

Further Reading

The Burmese Cat. Dorothy Silkstone Richards, Robine Pocock, Moira Swift, Vic Watson, Batsford 1975. Out of print but currently being revised.

Printed by Rapide Design & Print, Watton, Thetford, Norfolk, England.

Moira Swift

Sadly Moira Swift died in 1986 and did not live to see this book published. In her lifetime she was a valuable member of the Cat Fancy. Moira served on the Burmese Cat Club Committee for many years and she was often seen judging Burmese at cat shows. Her breeding prefix, Sabra, which she owned jointly with Marguerite Silverman will be found in many a Burmese Pedigree.

Moira Swift with two of her Blue Burmese, Debbie & Rosie.

Robine Pocock & Christina Payne wish to dedicate

this book to Moira's memory.

Introduction & Prologue

This book is not just another picture book of cats, but an attempt by the photographers and authors to show you that intangible mystique and appeal which makes many people each year introduce a Burmese into their homes and creates heartbreak for those who lose one from old age or accident but who would never have a cat of any other breed.

Burmese appeal is worldwide, although standards of appearance differ from one country to another. In Britain they are second in popularity only to Siamese, are being shown in increasingly large numbers and live in an ever growing number of homes. At the time of writing, for instance, the Burmese Cat Club of the UK has the largest membership of any club in the country. Founded in 1955 with a membership of just over 50, it had grown by 1989 to over 1500.

These photographs show Burmese cats as they are and look, and doing the thing Burmese do. Not all the Burmese in these pictures may be outstanding examples of their type (and the quick eye of the American breeder will soon spot some differences between these British-bred cats and their own stock), but this book is primarily about their inimitable character, not their show points. The vast majority of owners after all, look on their Burmese as much-loved pets, not show cats cherished for their physical perfection.

Many people think of Burmese only as brown cats; this book has some surprises in store for them, for there are nine other hues genetically possible in the Burmese rainbow. Whatever their colour, though, these cats all possess the unique characteristics of the breed - intelligence, affection, mischief, athletic ability and loyalty to humans. Tough, vital and fearless, these endearing creatures are indeed sometimes a little too full of curiosity and adventure, and the hilarious scrapes into which they sometimes get themselves will be familiar to most owners.

For those who own, or are owned by, a Burmese cat, we hope this book will serve as a reminder of playful kittenhood, adult magnificence and old age serenity. For the rest, perhaps it will act as a spur to join the ranks of those already enslaved by these lovable companions.

Before you look at the pictures, those of you who have owned a Burmese may have read previous books on the subject, and therefore will have some idea about how they originated, but for those who have not, we will give you an outline.

In America, the story began in 1930 when Wong Mau, a shorthaired brown female cat of eastern type, was brought from Burma to San Francisco by a gentleman named Dr. Joseph C. Thompson. Dr. Thompson was a retired ship's doctor of the US Navy who by all accounts was a flamboyant and intriguing character. He was deeply interested in the East, becoming at one stage, it is said, a Buddhist monk in a Lama monastery in Tibet, and once back in the States must have been a notable sight with his taste for Eastern clothes and jewellery. On a less unorthodox note, he was also noted for his work on marine fauna.

The story goes that he obtained Wong Mau from Frank 'Bring 'em back alive' Buck, a renowned collector of wild animals. It is said that Buck happened on the little cat when she was on exhibition at a native carnival in Rangoon. By the time Wong Mau came into his life, Thompson had established a psychiatry practice at his bungalow in San Francisco. Here he also bred cats, though not, as will be seen, merely as a hobby. The doctor chose his patients carefully (a good few of them were the wives of successful business men) and his cats were required to participate in the therapy. Patients would often find themselves leaving the surgery accompanied by a pregnant Siamese, it being Dr Thompson's theory that raising a litter of these lively creatures would banish all their other troubles from mind.

Wong Mau had a special place in Dr Thompson's affections, and she became a familiar sight at his consultations, perched regally at his side. In those days, Siamese had shorter heads and a slight nosebreak, rather than the triangular shape and straight profile that is required today; neither did they have such a distinctive whip tail, and American cat fanciers of the day took Wong Mau to be nothing more remarkable than an unusually dark-coated Siamese. Thompson, however, having compared her with his own Siamese, realised that there were some marked differences in type. A small, fine-boned cat, Wong Mau was rather more compact in body with a shorter tail, rounded widely-spaced eyes and a domed short-muzzled head without any sign of a pinch. Reports vary as to her eye-colour - some say golden, other turquoise - but all are agreed on the darkness of her points compared to her body colour, indicating that Wong Mau was in fact a Burmese-Siamese hybrid.

Hoping to shed light on Wong Mau's genetic make-up, Dr Thompson persuaded three of his breeder and geneticist friends, Virginia C. Cobb, Clyde E. Keeler and Madeleine Dmytryk, to co-operate with him in a series of breeding experiments. As there was no other cat of the same breed with which to mate her, Wong Mau's first husband was a Siamese, Tai. Two types of kittens resulted. One was typically Siamese in every respect; the other identical to Wong Mau, with her brown coat and darker points. When one of the latter was mated back to Wong Mau, three types of kittens resulted - some Siamese, some brown with points, and some solid brown with little or no darkening of ears, tail, feet or mask. When these solid brown cats were mated together, only solid brown kittens were produced. The detective work of Dr. Thompson and his colleagues had paid off handsomely. They had proved beyond doubt that the Burmese was a distinct breed with a sound genetic basis.

Where did Wong Mau and her ancestors originate? A romantic legend - alas unsubstantiated - is that she was stolen from a remote temple. Conjecture is that she was of the same strain as the little 'Rajah' cats described later by Major Finch, an Army Officer stationed in the East during World War II, in the January 1948 issue of CATS magazine. Contrary to popular belief of the time, Major Finch, who himself brought a female Burmese 'Simbuni' back to the United States, maintained that these 'Rajah', or Burmese cats were a recognised breed out there. During the war, on visits to Buddhist temples, he is reputed to have seen many outstandingly beautiful examples of these cats. The 'Rajahs', he learned, were the pets of the head priest or abbot and were held in great esteem - so much so that they were each assigned a young student priest whose duties ran to indulging every whim of these fortunate creatures. Major Finch also held that these Burmese 'Rajahs' were the traditional pets of Royalty long before the Siamese lorded it over the Royal Court of Siam. Treasured by these kings of ancient times, they were treated as four-footed members of the Royal Family.

According to Major Finch, Rajah fanciers in Burma also believed that the Siamese actually developed from an Albino Burmese pair exported from their country. This is an interesting reversal of the rather more conventional theory that the Burmese was at one stage a 'sport' or brown Siamese mutation.

Despite the fact that Dr Thompson and his colleagues had proved that the Burmese belonged to a newly-discovered true-breeding variety, the road to its recognition and development in the United States was by no means an easy one. The breed was first recognised by the American Cat Fanciers' Association (CFA) in 1936 and in the decade that followed Burmese began to achieve major successes at shows. Then, however, came a harsh setback when the CFA suspended its recognition. Many years later, we can only speculate why it happened, but at the root of the problem seems to have been the small number of pure-bred cats available and the necessity of out-crossing them with Siamese. From articles which appeared in magazines at the time, it appeared, too, that some breeders had genuine difficulty in distinguishing between pure Burmese and Burmese/Siamese hybrids and that a few others deliberately exploited this confusion by producing hybrids and passing them off as wholly Burmese. Fortunately, in the long run this seemingly devasting setback did little but good for the breed, for it made responsible breeders even more determined to extend and improve their stock. Indeed, it was during this period of exile that Sin Gu of Forbidden City and So Wat of Forbidden City, both significant in British pedigrees, were produced. Finally, in 1953, the CFA were sufficiently reassured by the development of the breed to restore its recognition.

It is hardly surprising, since Dr Thompson was a resident of San Francisco, that the breed's early progress unfolded on the West coast of America. From here came Dr Thompson's Mau Cats, the Gerstdale Burmese of Mrs Billie Gerst and Mrs Alexander's prefix of Mrs Mildred Alexander. Other names which subsequently figured in these early pedigrees (perhaps you can trace your American Burmese back to them) are The Farm, Forbidden City, Casa Gatos (from the West Coast) and, from the East Coast, Newton, Chindwin, Laos and Yana, Tang Wong, Cummings and Miss Burns. What a mixture of the practical and the romantic!

Another important link in the British Burmese chain is Chango of The Farm, bred by Miss Winifred Porter. He was a Burmese/Siamese hybrid, bred in 1941 who was later mated with a Siamese female belonging to the Cames Laos and Yana cattery. The Cames gave up breeding around 1950 and most of their stock passed to Mr & Mrs Warren of Idyllwild, Cailfornia. The story doesn't end there but the rest will be told when we come to Burmese in Britain.

Up to 1958 East & West had had their own separate breed associations, but that year they amalgamated to form the United Burmese Cat Fanciers. It was a significant marriage from the point of view of the subsequent development of the American Burmese. Up till then, the original American standard of points as recognised by CFA required a cat of foreign type - more like the sort bred in England today. In 1959 though, this standard was considerably changed by the UBCF. Now, to us on this side of the Atlantic at any rate, the Burmese in America tends more towards a cat of domestic short-hair type, with compact appearance, shorter legs, rounded feet, fuller head and round eyes. The British, meanwhile, still prefer their Burmese to be of foreign type though not tending towards to-day's "typey" Siamese. Why worry? Both shapes make beautiful cats.

Interestingly, the Burmese story in Great Britain opens very early indeed - around the turn of the century. Frances Simpson, writing in 1903, describes two exisitng types of Siamese cat of the time. The 'Royal Cat of Siam', cream-coloured, dark-pointed and sapphire-eyed, was obviously the forerunner of our present-day Siamese, and was more popular than the other kind, the more subtly shaded Chocolate. These Chocolates, however, were described in detail by various well-known breeders of the day. They were identical to the Royals in all aspects except body colour. A deep brown with hardly any markings, though not all descriptions tallied when it came to eye colour. While some fanciers wrote of them as having blue eyes, Mr Harrison Weir, a noted breeder, recorded in 1889 that his chocolate Siamese had eyes of 'a rich amber colour', and the clear picture which emerges from the descriptions of these early breeders is of a dark-bodied cat with some intensification of hue in the points and variable eye colour, sometimes blue, sometimes yellow. A mystery? Not really. All these observed facts can be satisfactorily explained by the hypothesis that these early chocolate Siamese were actually Burmese/Siamese hybrids like Wong Mau.

It seems, therefore, that the cats like Wong Mau were known in Britain as long ago as 1889. But with their dark coats at the time less fashionable than the more immediately striking colour of the 'Royal' Siamese, they were passed over and we owe it to Dr Thompson and the other dedicated American breeders that the unique Burmese is delighting us today.

So the British development of the Burmese did not truly begin till more than half a century later. For that, we must be grateful to Mr & Mrs S. France of Derby. Even now, importing and developing a new breed of cat involves risk and expense as well as the very real possibility of disappointment. In 1949, when American Burmese was in its early days as a breed and moreover bereft of its recognition by the CFA, it was a brave decision indeed, particularly since travelling arrangements were so much more difficult to organise then and quarantine facilities so much poorer. How would these imported cats react to their journey and the colder, damper climate of their new country? There were going to be problems, but the Frances persevered.

With the Chinki prefix, Mrs France was already noted as a breeder of Siamese, so she had at least many years of experience as a breeder to help in the task that lay ahead. Their interest having been aroused in Burmese, it was Mrs Blanche Warren of Idyllwild, California whom the Frances first contacted. It was a good choice. From California came Chindwins Minou Twm and Ch.(USA) Laos Cheli Wat (both females) and the male Casa Gatos da Foong, all three unrelated and of the best breeding then available in the United States. Cheli, who like da Foong, had a hybrid mother, had won her American championship under the CFF in 1948, having been best of colour and best Burmese in the CFF Brooklyn Long Island Cat Club Show the year before. She and Minou were mated to two different males before they left for their new life.

Cheli, unfortunately, was found subsequently not to be pregnant but Minous' litter was born in quarantine at Tamworth in Staffordshire. Here came another set-back. The Frances found out, too late, that kittens born in quarantine could be taken out before the mother had ended her six month quarantine period enforced in the UK. With Minou quite badly affected by the change of climate, the kittens sad to say, did not survive. Mrs France was left without kittens from either queen and thus a considerable whittling down of the breeding lines which she might have had available to her.

Poor Minou, indeed, never really recovered from the respiratory troubles which had ailed her in confinement, but she did leave one litter behind her to carry on her line. Of that litter, Chinki Yong Zahran, a male, was mated as an adult to Ch.Laos Cheli Wat to produce Chinki Yong Jetta, Britain's first champion brown Burmese. Zahran's litter sister Chinki Yong Kassa, mated to Casa Gatos da Foong, produced another champion in Sablesilk Bimbo.

Known to his intimates as Daffy, Casa Gatos da Foong was the first Burmese to be introduced to the British public. Mrs France exhibited him at the Croydon Cat Club Show in Hammersmith, London in November 1949 and he later appeared on television. The public were enchanted with these confident, playful and handsome brown cats and kittens who within a short space of time were appearing at more and more shows. The Burmese were on their way at last to becoming Britain's second most popular breed, after Siamese.

Largely perhaps, because the CFA of America had suspended recognition of the Burmese at the time, the Governing Council of the Cat Fancy (GB), would not give breed recognition on the strength of the American pedigrees and stipulated proof of three generations of pure breeding in Britain. The first of these third-generation litters arrived in 1952 thanks to Chinki Yong Shwegalay, owned by Dr Attwell of Sheffield. The GCCF gave breed recognition shortly afterwards.

However, failure of Minou and Cheli to provide kittens from their pre-import matings was proving rather a problem, as it seriously limited the variety of bloodlines breeders needed if the British Burmese were to continue and improve. Again it was Mrs Blanche Warren who provided the answer, in the shape of Casa Gatos Darkee, an American Burmese male who was to play a great part in the subsequent development of the Burmese in Britain.

Darkee arrived in England in 1953. Less than a year later, when Mrs France was forced for domestic reasons to give up her Burmese, he and the other three imported cats were taken over by the late Mrs C.F Watson of Matlock, together with Chinki Yong Jetta who was in kitten to Darkee, the mating that would eventually produce the mother of the first Blue Burmese.

By 1956 it is safe to say that the Burmese had truly arrived. The Burmese Cat Club had been inaugurated with more than 50 founder members, many well-known breeders were starting lines of their own, and already there were eight full show champions, (including Chinki Yong Jetta) and one full premier. British Burmese had been exported to Kenya, New Zealand, Ceylon, Canada, Eire, Scandinavia, Australia and South Africa. However, it was already becoming obvious that if the breed was to continue its expansion and improvement, new blood would again have to be introduced.

Darshan Khudiram, who was an East Coast cat and vastly different in pedigree from the previously imported West Coast stock, was brought to England by Mrs C.F. Watson in 1957. Soon after this, Mrs Watson also had the good luck to acquire, quite by chance,Folly Tou-Po, another American-bred cat, from a Canadian who had been living in Britain. These six imported cats make up the roll of honour of the original breeding stock for British-bred Burmese. Then in 1969, Dr. Elaine Allen returned from Canada with her English bred brown queen, Dormin Pysche, and two half Canadian cats, a male, Tapawingo Tahltan and a female, Tapawingo Beothuk. Pysche had been mated to Ch. Wai-Ling of Fredna's thus producing Beothuk and the second mating to Gr. Ch. Halton Ridge Alfie, produced Tahltan, who became a Champion. Beothuk also produced another litter in quarantine by Wai-Ling. So far we have only been talking about one single colour, the brown. But in 1955 began the story of Blue Burmese. That mating, previously mentioned, between Casa Gatos Darkee and Ch. Chinki Yong Jetta, produced a female named Chinki Golden Gay. In due course, Gay was mated back to her father, Darkee and presented her owner, Mrs Watson, with a litter of six kittens.

While Gay's kittens were being born at Matlock, it so happened that in nearby Leicester, Mrs Margaret Smith's Chinki Yong Kassa was also on the production line. Kassa though produced only a single kitten, but she was a confident, experienced mother whereas Gay was a young cat coping with her first litter. Their two owners, close friends, decided to alter slightly the sizes of the family units. Accordingly, two of Gay's large family went to the motherly Kassa, who immediately accepted them and successfully brought them up.

There was a surprise in store. Gay's two kittens, a male and a female, had been the same colour at birth, but as the girl grew her coat began to lighten till at four weeks it was a light silvery grey. In 1955, when knowledge of genetics was not as widespread as it is now, this little kitten's pale blue coat must have come as a disturbing puzzle to breeders engaged in producing a line of brown cats who were supposed to be breeding true. Now we know that there is a simple explanation. As previously explained, it was necessary to use Siamese in the early days of building Burmese stock. Possibly unknown to breeders at that time, some of the Siamese used for the purpose carried the blue (diluted brown) gene. If so, that blue gene might well have been passed to the Burmese/Siamese hybrid and then to a pure Burmese cat. All it needed was a mating between two Burmese both carrying this respective blue factor for a blue kitten to make its appearance. In other words, if Darkee had been carrying blue in this way, he could have passed it on to Gay, who, whilst also having the normal brown appearance could carry the blue gene. Once father and daughter were mated, those two blue genes would combine to produce the blue kitten. She was aptly named Sealcoat Blue Surprise, and turned out to be a beautiful cat with a lovely disposition. She died in 1971. Several breeders were attracted to this new colour and the number of blue cats slowly increased. By 1960 they were recognised by the GCCF with championship status.

With the arrival of the Blue Burmese, breeders became interested in the possibility of yet more colour variations. Around 1959, in America, some paler-coated brown cats had been observed in litters. They were apparently cats in which the normal brown gene of the Burmese (genetically equivalent to black) had been replaced by a genetic brown which appeared as a milky chocolate colour. It occured to breeders that these light cats were akin to chocolate-pointed Siamese, and if this were so a blue-diluted version could be obtained. This did in fact turn out to be the case. In America these light browns became known as champagnes and their blue-diluted counterparts as platinums. In Britain we know them as chocolate and lilac. All these new varieties of Burmese have achieved breed recognition in Britain and in America, although the CFA recognises them under the name of Malayans. In 1964 came the introduction of even newer colours in Britain, namely the reds, creams and torties. Here it is necessary to remember that red is a sex-linked colour - i.e reds (and the blue-dilute form, cream) can be either male or female cats, but torties, except very rarely, are females. In fact, the production of these colours began by accident, when a blue Burmese female escaped and eloped with a short-haired red tabby.

Breeders' curiosity was sufficiently aroused for a breeding programme to be undertaken. From this first accidental mating of the blue Burmese and the red tabby was a very lithe and elegant black and red tortie of foreign type. Meanwhile, a brown Burmese female had been deliberately mated to a red-pointed Siamese, and a tortie Burmese/Siamese hybrid from this alliance would be used for further breeding. A third line was established when a tortie moggie (carrying Siamese) was mated to a brown Burmese carrying blue, and a male kitten was kept.

Despite the hard work, expense and occasional misfortune (one litter was lost with cat flu when three weeks old) breeders triumphed eventually in producing red, cream and tortie cats identical in personality and appearance to the more traditional browns - typical Burmese, in fact. By 1973, the creams had championship status, and last of all, the torties were given it in 1977.

So now we have given you a little background reading and insight into this wonderful breed of cat. All that now remains is for you, the reader to sit back and enjoy the pictures which follow.

In the beginning..............

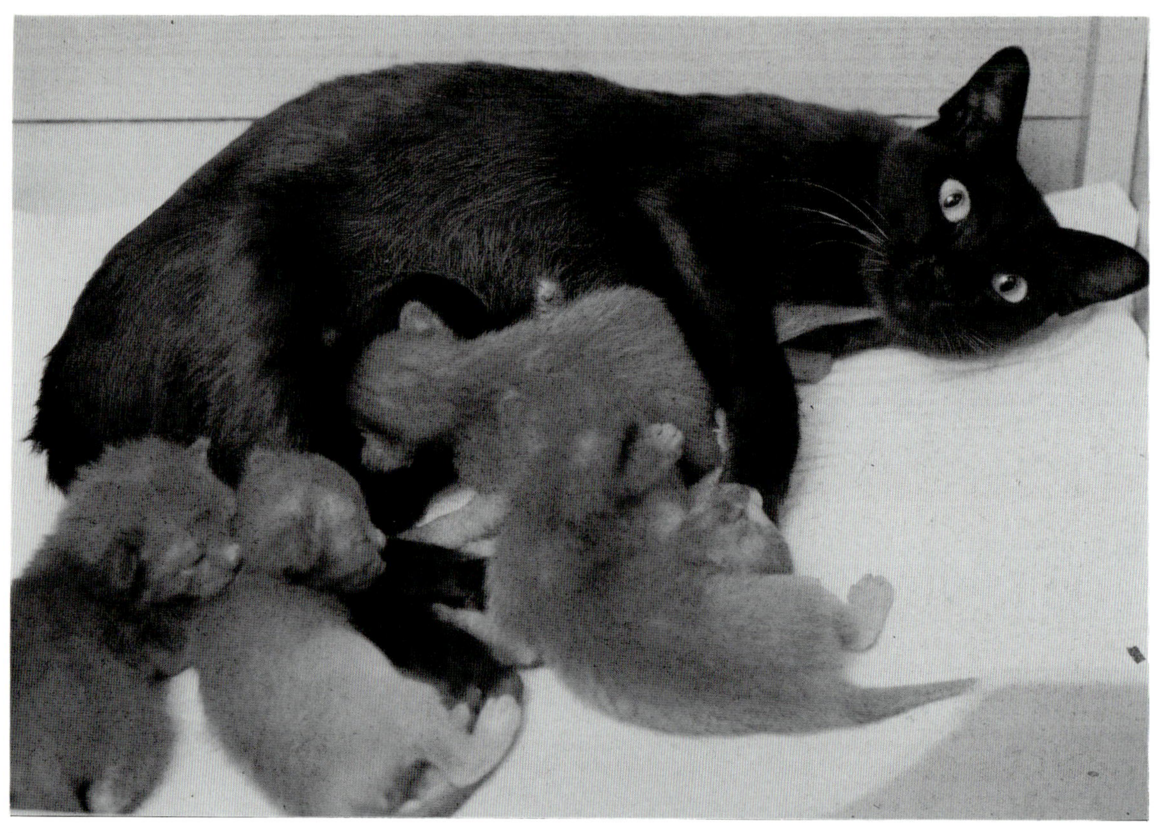

Burmese queens make wonderful mothers, and kittens begin life with lots of attention from the cat family

Perchance to dream.....
"Wakey, Wakey" says mum!

......including Dad sometimes,

Grannies & Aunts can help....

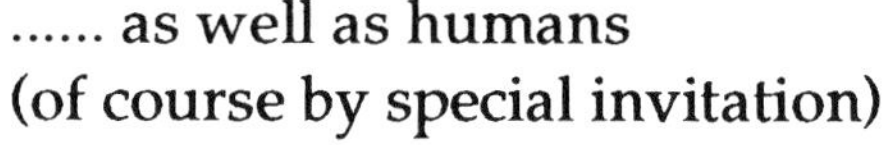

...... as well as humans
(of course by special invitation)

Families are often big - litters of seven or eight are frequent - and the queen will feed them quite happily,

Milk-bar time!

sometimes even sharing their bed with a friend ... in this case a Siamese

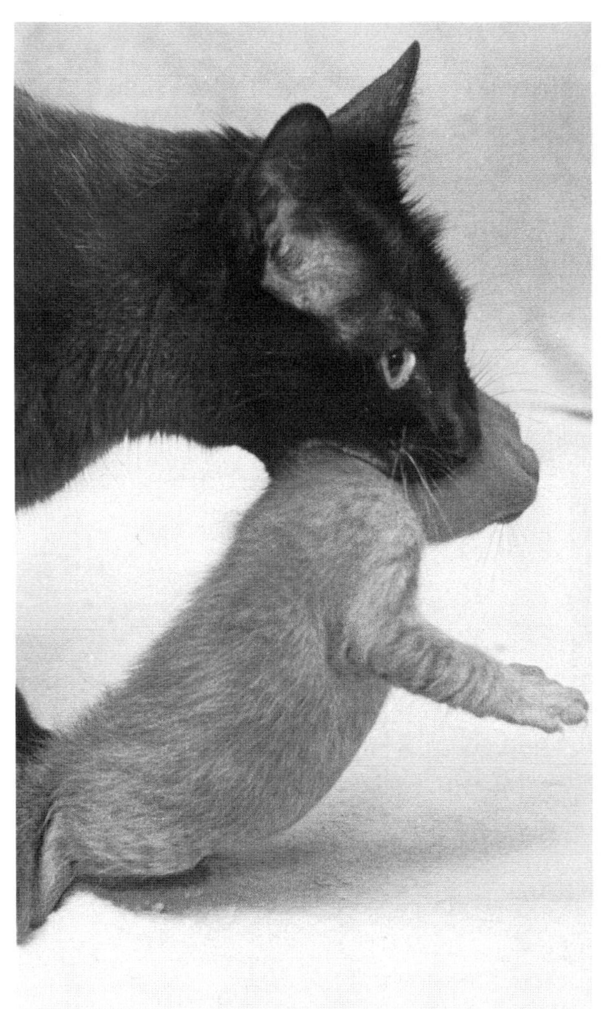

Most Burmese will not want to keep their babies where YOU want them, e.g., in the kittening box, or a special room, but can be very persistent about moving them where THEY want them, in your wardrobe, on top of a cupboard, etc. They have a wonderful knack of finding the most inconvenient place. At least as far as the owner is concerned!

Burmese can be very violent in the protection of their kittens,........but they love to show them off.......

Owners of Burmese will derive great pleasure watching their kittens grow up. From about four weeks of age the kittens develop rapidly, clumsy at first but quickly gaining confidence and expertise. The first skill usually acquired even before a kitten can walk, is learning to wash itself, copying mum but soon learning to do its own thing.

.......all good "Brownies" go to heaven

Creams don't need bibs at lunchtime.......

I'm Brown so is my Dad

Reds under the Bed?

Chocolate & Brown....girls about town

Tiny kittens will take well to being handled early, (providing mum approves), and early human contact will help to form the "human bond".

In fact other members of the house-hold will soon form friendly relationships with the new arrivals.

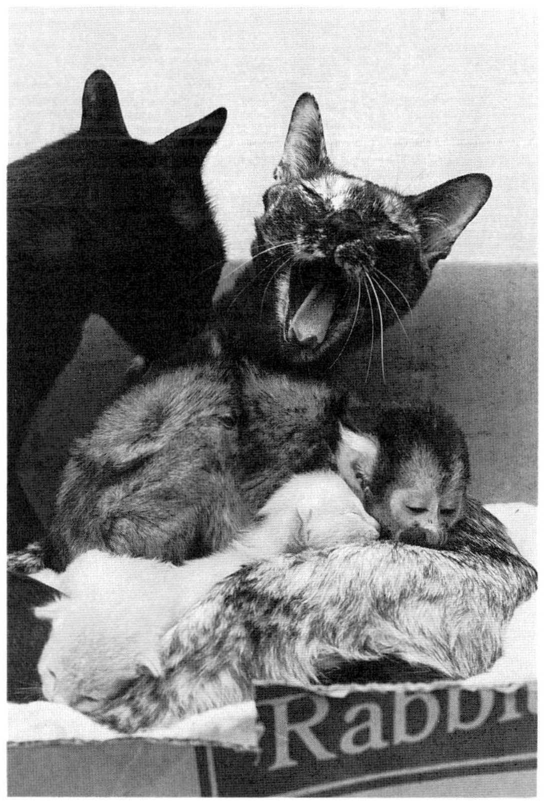

Mum is often the first target of play and she will endure happily all sorts of torments from her "horrors".

Almost instinctively they will learn to use a litter tray. Very young kittens will concentrate quite hard on the job in hand and will also take great delight in eating the clean litter or throwing it all over the place!

Older Kittens (and cats of course) will groom themselves constantly enjoying every moment.

Pet Mince?

"Will you never learn to leave things alone?"

"..and for your next lesson"

Christmas is a great time!

Bottoms Up!

Piano Forte!

I will kill it .... eventually.

He is always biffing me .....

Burmese have many games to delight you. One such game is called "Let's play Toilet Rolls!" and it goes like this ......

First, we roll it a little ...

... then we tug it a little. "You're doing fine, Son" ...

... then we pull a little harder ...

... Bingo!!

Many Burmese discover at quite an early age that the best way to get you to play with them is to retrieve. They will bring a toy back to you again and again, sometimes putting their paws around your ankles if you don't throw it promptly. Another great game is "Hide and Seek"; you do the hiding and they do the seeking.

Many are masters at opening lever handled doors and some can even turn lights on. It can be a little disconcerting to come home and find doors open and lights blazing when you had left everything closed up and in darkness.

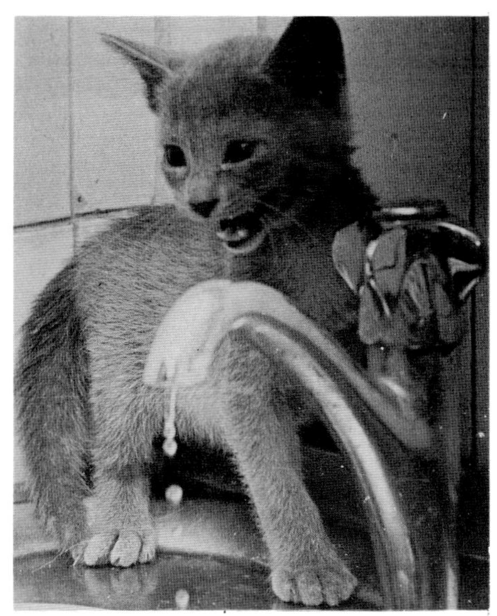

Beware ....
.... Burmese!

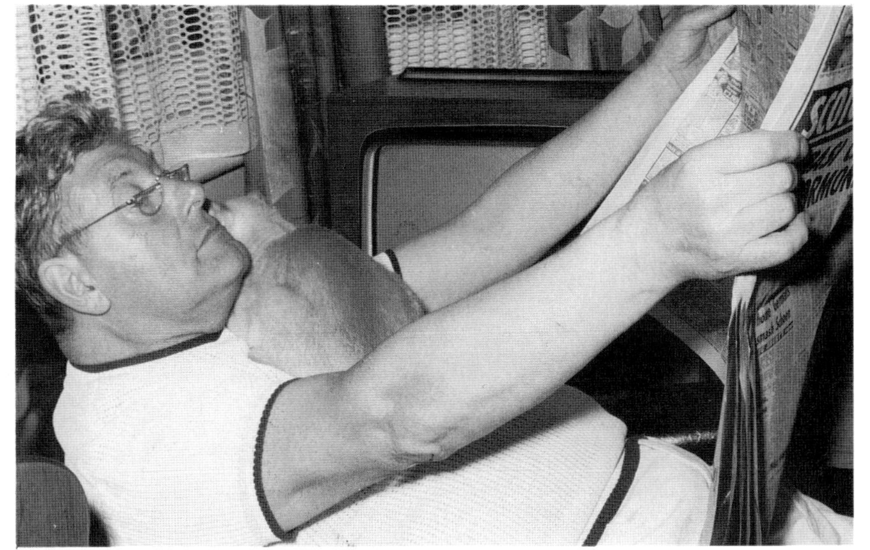

"If you thought you were going to ...

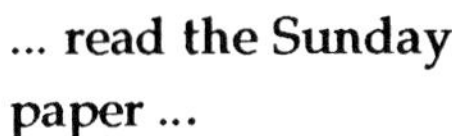

... read the Sunday paper ...

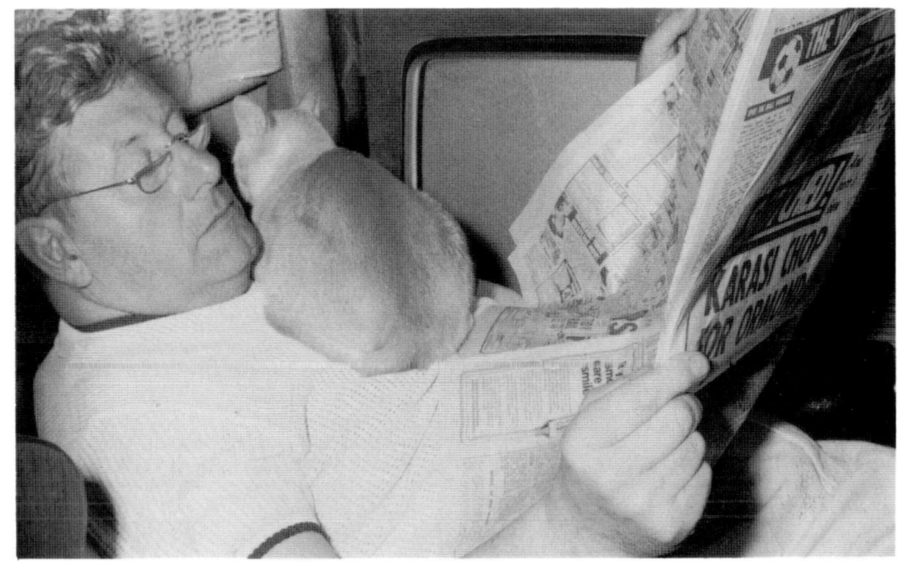

... then think again, Dad!"

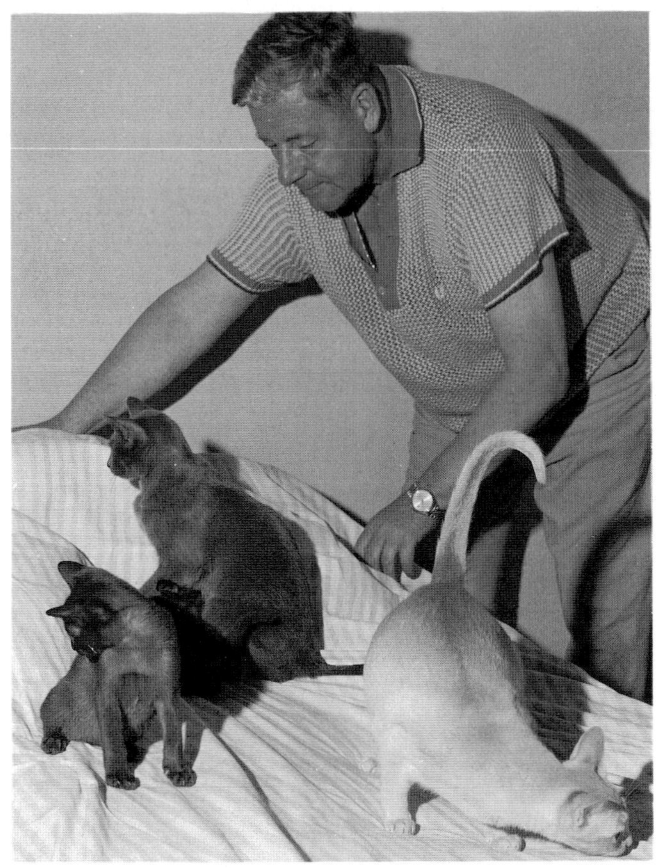

Burmese give bedmaking a whole new dimension!

Burmese will usually come when called or whistled, if it is convenient at the time for them to do so! Some will recognise your car and come to greet you on your arrival home from work. Mothers of young children need not fear Burmese, but, the cats will stand up for themselves if pushed too far!

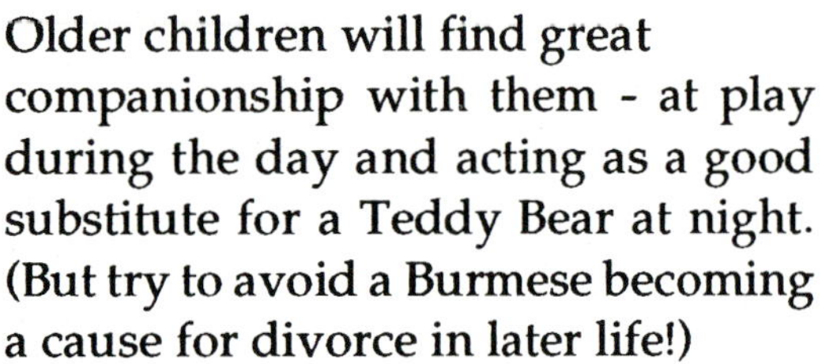

Older children will find great companionship with them - at play during the day and acting as a good substitute for a Teddy Bear at night. (But try to avoid a Burmese becoming a cause for divorce in later life!)

It is not easy to keep one step ahead of a Burmese; they have a cunning knack of outwitting you. A favourite trick is to disappear at bed-time if there is any likelihood of their being shut up in the kitchen for the night, and what better place to hide than under your bed - right in the middle? By the time you are on all fours trying to reach the cat at one side, he is on the other and vice versa. When you have given up and crawled into bed - exhausted , your cat will emerge and slither down between the sheets to join you, the give-away being a self-satisfied purr. Of course this doesn't happen often. A Burmese owner soon realises that the easiest line of resistance is to have the dear feline in bed in the first place (hence the divorce warning earlier) or get a cat less demanding in its choice of bedding.

'When cats run home and light is come
And dew is on the ground.'

Tennyson Song: The Owl

Indoors they will climb everything, including your Chippendale - but give them a scratching post and they will leave your furniture alone - usually.

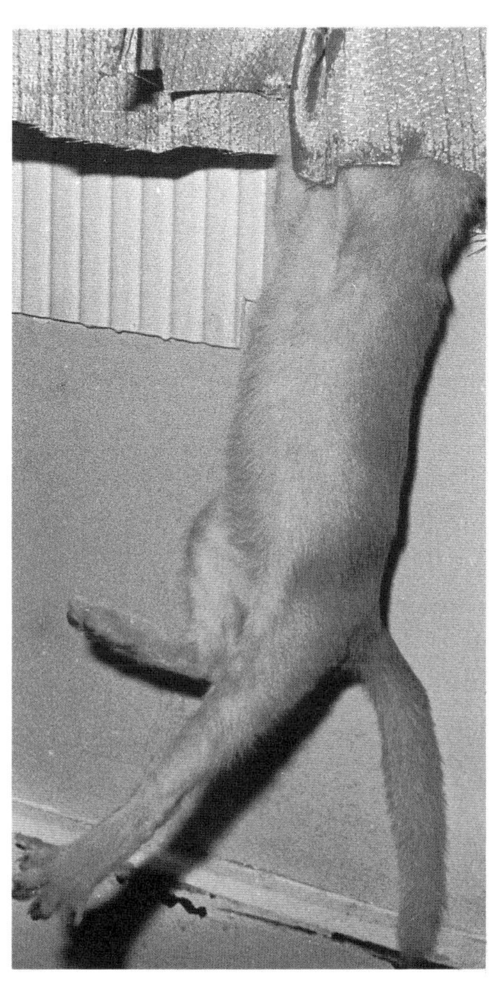

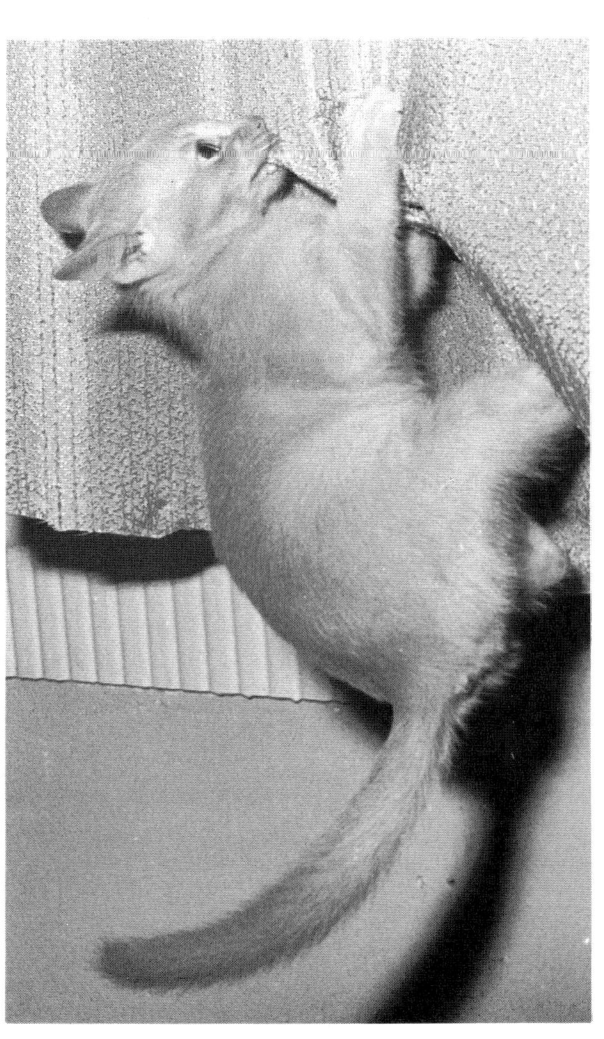

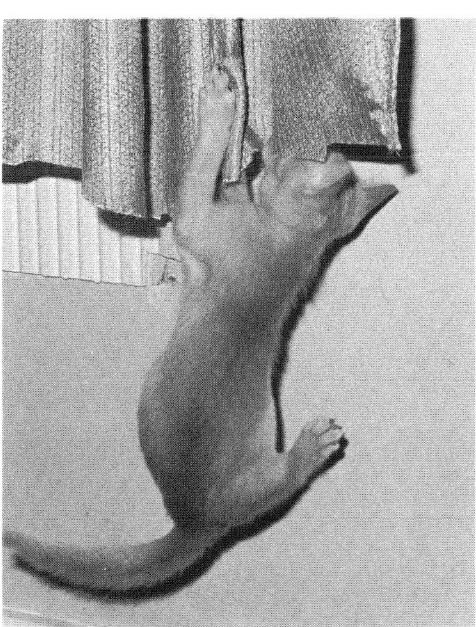

'Let the curtains fall ...
So let us welcome Peaceful evening in.'

Cowper: The Winter Evening

... and even in old age some will still be able to leap to the top of the door.

They are great comedians; one sometimes feels they jump in a bath full of water or fall down the loo purposely on their wild escapades. Their athleticism is combined with grace and charm, performing dances which will keep you spell-bound for hours - give them a ball or a toy mouse and see what happens. Their movements are so characteristic ......

"I would be there
Were it but to see how the
cat jumps."

Scott ib 7 Oct. 1826

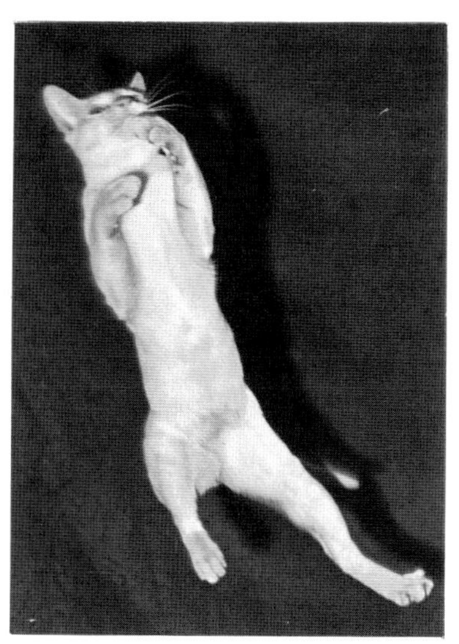

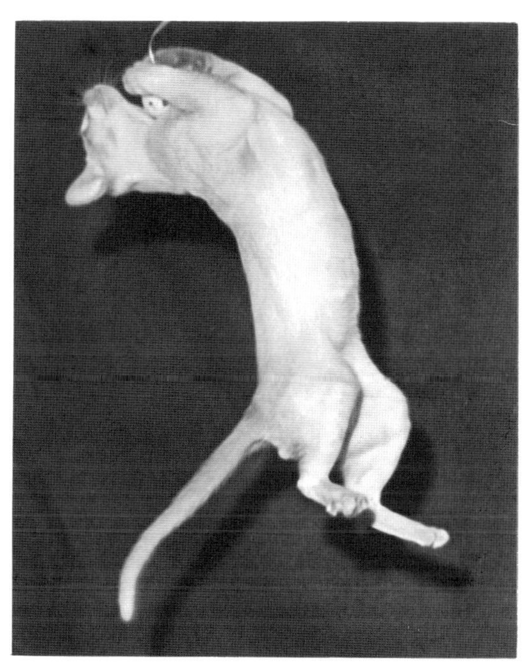

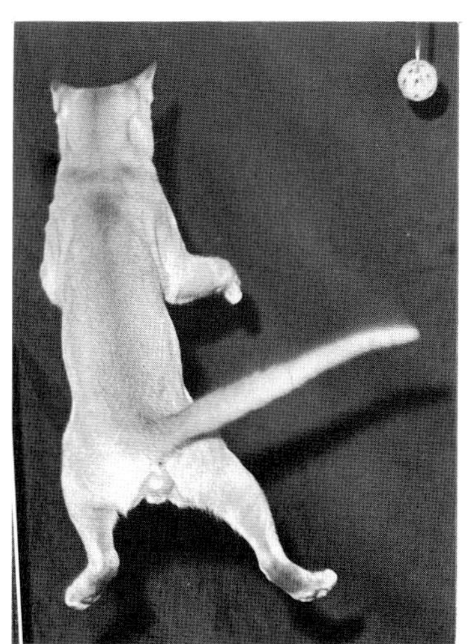

Burmese love to make friends with other animals, perhaps taking a little time to feel really confident, but making it in the end and often ultimately becoming the boss.

"Merely innocent flirtation,
Not quite adultery, but adulteration."

Byron: Don Juan

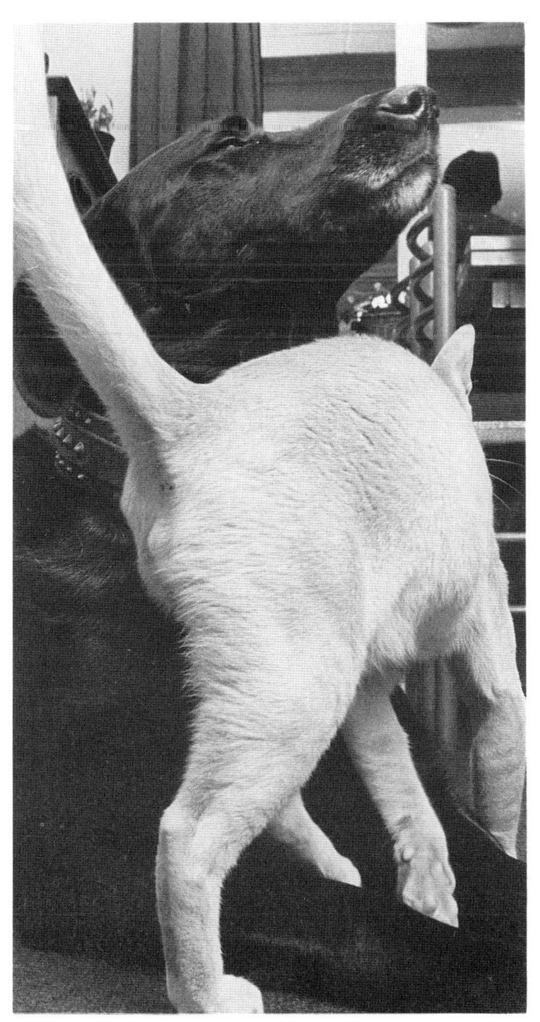

'O Cat of Churlish kind,
The fiend was in thy mind,
When though my bird untwined.'

Skelton ib.

"A bit of shaggy carpet thinks it's stealing my food ....but only because I've had all I want!"

"Hi, Chaps!"

"Cats and monkeys, monkeys and cats
-All human life is there."

Henry Jones: The Madonna of Future

Usually Burmese are quite fearless, and they are great hunters. Rabbits and pheasants as large as themselves are often their quarry.

"My brother may think he's conquered it ....

..... but I'm going to investigate further!"

"I know I'm beautiful - you needn't tell me!"

Blue - the sky's the limit

I could have been, Blue, Chocolate or Lilac,
but I happen to be Brown....Tortie of course!

Lilac Time!

Pals

Some Mothers do 'ave 'em!

Burmese do not mind travelling and will enjoy all modes of transport

..... they will even take to a harness.

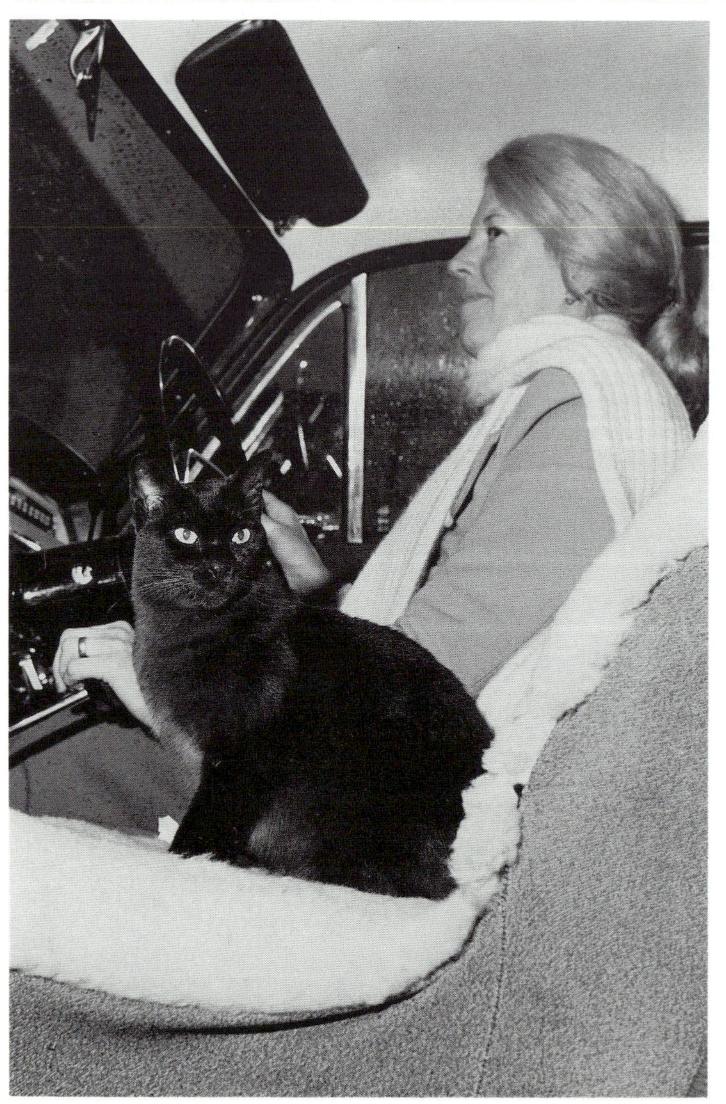

..... and cars are just great ...

Regretfully they may get lost this way as they sometimes jump into a stranger's car and get carried away for some distance. So it is a good idea to put an elastic collar on your cat with an identification disc.

Three generations of Blue Burmese

'A thing of beauty is a joy forever:
Its loveliness increases; it will never pass into nothingness.'

Keats

Although hardy, they love their comforts and appreciate warmth. They make ideal pets for flats, but in places where it is advisable to protect them from hazards of the roads, they should have access to fresh air having a wired window, balcony or run.

"Ouch, you're squashing me!" -- They love the sunshine and will follow the sun patches as they move across the carpet, seeking "a place in the sun".

"Oh, let the sunshine in"

Burmese grow to old age very beautifully and with great dignity. They never lose their appeal.

We have decided to name the cats you will now see. Some were very famous in their day and lots of you will remember them with great affection. Most of the pictures were taken when the cats were in their senior years.

Champion Belcanto Floria Tosca (Blue)

Champion Buskins Blue Sunya (Blue)

Champion Kingsplay Pollyana (Brown)

Arboreal Sitta (Brown)

Elboro Van (Brown)

Champion Braeside Golden Promise (Cream)

Champion Tapawingo Tahltan (Brown)

Champion Kalos Castor (Brown)

'I will consider my cat Jeoffry,
For he is the servant of the Living God
Duly and daily serving Him'

Smart Jubilate, Agno XIX

EPILOGUE

Champion Copplestone Lun-Tha

"Am writing an essay on the life-histories of insects
And have abandoned the idea of writing on 'How Cats Spend their Time'."

Barbellion: The Journal of a Disappointed Man, Jan. 1903.